Norman Friskney

VERSATILE VERSE

A collection of poems inspired by the
corridors of Oxford and the battlefields of Italy

Norman Friskney

VERSATILE VERSE

A collection of poems inspired by the
corridors of Oxford and the battlefields of Italy

MEREO
Cirencester

By the same author

With Gun & Gown

Mereo Books

1A The Wool Market Dyer Street Cirencester Gloucestershire GL7 2PR
An imprint of Memoirs Publishing www.mereobooks.com

VERSATILE VERSE: 978-1-909874-61-9

First published in Great Britain in 2015
by Mereo Books, an imprint of Memoirs Publishing

Copyright ©2015

Norman Friskney has asserted his ight under the Copyright Designs and Patents
Act 1988 to be identified as the author of this work.

This book is a work of fiction and except in the case of historical fact any resemblance to
actual persons living or dead is purely coincidental.

A CIP catalogue record for this book is available from the British Library.

This book is sold subject to the condition that it shall not by way of trade or otherwise be lent,
resold, hired out or otherwise circulated without the publisher's prior consent in any form of
binding or cover, other than that in which it is published and without a similar condition,
including this condition being imposed on the subsequent purchaser.

The address for Memoirs Publishing Group Limited can be found at
www.memoirspublishing.com

The Memoirs Publishing Group Ltd Reg. No. 7834348

The Memoirs Publishing Group supports both The Forest Stewardship Council® (FSC®) and the
PEFC® leading international forest-certification organisations. Our books carrying both the FSC
label and the PEFC® and are printed on FSC®-certified paper. FSC® is the only
forest-certification scheme supported by the leading environmental organisations including
Greenpeace. Our paper procurement policy can be found at
www.memoirspublishing.com/environment

Typeset in 9/15pt Bembo
by Wiltshire Associates Publisher Services Ltd. Printed and bound in Great Britain by
Printondemand-Worldwide, Peterborough PE2 6XD

For Kathleen, with love

CONTENTS

Pie in the Sky
Posterity
That ye be not judged
Intimations of Mortality
Millennial Mayhem
For Anthony and Alan
More Fragile Than We Knew
It's Not What You Know
Human Conditional
Sweet Memory
Gaudy Night
A Cautionary Word for 18/21
Paradise Nearly Regained
A Widow's Hump
Social Insecurity
Name Dropping
Passport to Paradise
Primary Colours

The Trees
To Kathleen
Long Love
Per Amor Ad Astra
Better Than Rubies
The Sundial
For a Silver Wedding
The Usher's Tale
Forgive Me
To Lucy and Kiara on reaching 18
Ode to an ageing tennis player
Dancing
A visitation
The spinney
All flesh is as grass
Young love
The secret garden of flowers

INTRODUCTION

Versatile verse is a collection written over the years, in some instances for family and friends. Only two of these have been previously published in the Jesus College Oxford Record: 'Gaudy Night' and the requiem for 'Anthony and Alan'. These two were in the Officers' Training Corps with me in our first year at University. Edmund Blunden, the First World War poet, lectured the Corps in military map reading. Anthony served with me in 8th Army in Italy as infantry officers and Alan in France. Both were killed.

Few of the other verses require clarification. In 'It's Not What You Know' the 'Man' refers to the Headmaster at a very well-known public school. In 'Gaudy Night' Meyrick Scholarships were closed to Welsh undergraduates. In the same piece 'Collections' refers to the Oxford practice of a formal end of term assessment of work, not helped if the 'Battels Bill' for items like beer is excessive. 'Parsons' Pleasure' is a riverside retreat where, reputedly, naked dons disported themselves in the past. In 'Name Dropping' all the encounters actually took place except those with Beelzebub and Mephistopheles. 'The Usher's Tale' is a feeble attempt at Chaucerian style, and is entirely apocryphal. It was written for the amusement of dear friends, the clerk, a schoolmaster and his wife, a lecturer in art.

When Marlowe first in Tamburlaine
Made verses blank a splendid thing
He, the great metrist, set the stage
For soaring Shakespeare to take wing

Yet those of us in humbler vein
Wrestle with scansion and with rhyme
Not for us tennis with no net
Or court unmarked with service line.

Yet nor do we, as some today
Who scribble in recondite hand
Disgorge lines, he who writes himself
Cannot, perhaps, quite understand.

PIE IN THE SKY

Go forth, my son of seventeen summers long
The prophet calls you to this holy war
To shoulder pack and charge your friendly gun
The Imman knows what you are fighting for.
And blest are they who fall upon the field
Their path to paradise shall surely be
For them to tread where houries wait to yield
To him who heeds the Prophet's clerisy.

Once there were those who bore Crusaders' shields
And some devised th' inquisitorial rack
Whilst others who believed in 'Gott mit uns'
Could expiate the holocaust or sack
Of those who would not to their dogma yield
For deity had sanctified their fight
And know that ends will justify all means
Of they who have such certainty of right.

This is for you no bitter sacrifice
You are not now forsaken as I call
Upon you now to pay the simple price
For this you do for one and yet for all.
The two on either side shall shed their sin
And you the burden bear of guilt and vice
For surely you have pledged that they this night
Shall be beside you there in paradise.

For we are old, and old as time itself
And we hold all monopoly of truth
And woe who would deny our sophistry
Or dare to ask from us some shallow proof
That we are right: we know that we are right
Our banner and our flag proclaim our call
We will not rest until the final fight
For we are all in one and one in all.

POSTERITY

They say we are of native blood
We of these scattered Isles of Britain
Survivors of the flood when sol baked all
And northwards came the great migration,
The hungry hordes of robber bands
To occupy our land of Weald
As we set sail for Chiltern reef
Where rest we now till we are healed.

'Tis said that in Uralistan, and even in Alaskaland
Are places where one still can sit
In winter and enjoy the sun
And not live deep in caves like we.

Yet others say, beneath the sea
Which laps long shores of Alplands Isle
Are cities where in antique times
Lived those who in a golden age
Rode chariots like machines on wheels

And flew with birds about the sky.
One of their savants even wrote of us
And said in sorrow 'For our today
We traded your tomorrow'.

THAT YE BE NOT JUDGED

I wandered through the years long past
Dream drifting in the shades of night
That century that had been mine
Whose darkling clouds obscured the light.

And all around me there they stood
A great concourse of human kind
Old friends long gone and others still
I knew not, far in distant lines.

And there He sat upon the throne
'Free will I gave you and far more
Both life and death, health and disease
Food, hunger, concord yet and war.'

For I am Alpha, Omega
Jehovah, Lord omnipotent
First cause, creator absolute
All merciful, omniscient.

He set the scales before our eyes
Yet others from them fell away
As we assessed our human plight
Of debt we might be called to pay.

Glad to awake, the veil of night
Dissolved in morning's early ray
And yet, and yet I felt that we
Him wanting found on Judgement Day.

INTIMATIONS OF MORTALITY

I have been here before
Whilst reality slept in the womb of tomorrow
Which is today, the passing picture show
Flickering out its last few frames
Before the reinstatement of the void.
What I have known I will no longer know
Yet here attends no fear or sorrow
Just a closing of the door.

I have been there before
Oblivious of the yesteryears of time
Through endlessness that sparks into this present light
Whilst all around the galaxies were born and died
The heartbeat of the universe
Blossoming and fading into blackest night
Unknowable behind an adamantine
And yet unopened door.

I have been there before
And all who are today were there with me
We knew not, nor did one from other know
Yet passed into this light of common day
And then, held hand in hand together
In love and brotherhood until the stay

Was past and once again time met eternity
To close the door.

We have been there before
Return we not alone to that unknown
Where present, past and future meet
And all creation coalesce where time is not
Where harmony supplants the feared oblivion
And all is one where none compete
Avowing they alone unlock or keep the door.

Have we been there before?
There is no need for man's consistory
Transcending all we know or cannot know
Confounding all who dare presume
Unique and sole enlightenment of truth.
There but remains above, here and below
The enigma and the mystery
That lies behind the door.

MILLENNIAL MAYHEM

Our probe, Department Five of Planetary Ethnology
Stationed close to star B693
Has now recorded images of twenty hundred orbits
Around the sun of planet number three.

One species, newly dominant, emerging from the primitive
Can now receive transmissions visually
We are about to beam to them a thirty-year signal
Of past events, on shoreline east, the inland sea.

Our recordings are pellucid (we can read their hieroglyphics)
On our earlier tapes two thousand circuits back
Whilst events which then unfolded appear to have significance
Which codes our research teams soon hope to crack.

These include the deeds and words of a wandering ethnic preacher
Whose times we've documented in detail
We intend to transmit to them the more noteworthy pictures
Of his life in Palestine, now called Israel.

It is of the greatest interest to our ethnological departments
While observing the reactions of a species when at last
We send them information both literal and of substance
To enable them to view true graphic pictures of their past.

We anticipate consternation and indeed some agitation
As we override their information screens
And we will observe objectively their ethical reactions
As they try to come to terms with what this means.

It is our firm intention to eschew physical intervention
Should our images upset their social status quo
Our motives are as always scientific and objective
As our impeccable galactic records show.

FOR ANTHONY AND ALAN

Full fifty years have passed since when
Young freshmen in the Corps
At Blunden's feet at Qxford

VERSATILE VERSE

In those early days of war
We sat as he expounded
On compass work by night
'Freeze if they put a flare up
Don't move while it is light'
He'd seen lights he loved extinguished
Five and twenty years before
And he knew that which we then knew not
Of kinship forged in war
For in front line fraternity
In his turn he'd borne the cross
And knew that out of friendship
Comes the loving and the loss.

So as the shadows lengthened
That autumn afternoon
Whilst at his feet we listened
As he quoted Owen and Sassoon
We saw that something glistened
Beneath our mentor's eye
As mirrored in our youth he saw
Friends he had left to lie.
So with Alan and with Anthony
As I dined that night in hall
And talked of 'poor old Blunden'
We each knew that his recall
Of comradeships long shattered
On that anvil wrought anew
Might soon make our firmfast friendship
More fragile than we knew.

Guilt lingers with survivors
As the years roll soft away
And on the Jesus war memorial
Are the names of those whose day
Was so short and we like Blunden
Find our tears can't drown the lie
That dulce et decorem est pro patria mori.

IT'S NOT WHAT YOU KNOW

Yes, Pater knew the Provost well
And the Provost knew the Man
For the Provost was in Pop himself
And dad an Oppidan
But Common Entrance, Maths and Latin
I'd found too much to face
But it's who you know, not what you know,
So I passed and got a place.

To become a Commoner at Oxbridge
When Pater left the College
Matriculation was enough
To show sufficient knowledge
To tackle Schools or Tripos
And gain a pass degree
No nonsense then with UCCA forms
Or things like GCE.
So when in time it was my turn
To follow Pater there
He helped the College fund

VERSATILE VERSE

A Professorial chair
And at dinner on high table
At Gaudy night in May
Pledged gifts of wine from our estate
At Châteauneuf de Vezelay.

After years of dissipation
Poor Pater passed away
Left all of us so strapped for cash
And tax we couldn't pay
But I took his place up at the Lords
And tho' debates are such a bore
Attendance cash has been a lifeline
When the wolf is at the door

There is never any gratitude
For all that we have done
For generations since the Conquest
To ensure the country's run
By breeding and by blood line
Which has long suppressed revolt
And now we've had our place usurped
By those below the salt.

But when my time is come I'm sure
There'll always be some hope
For Pater knew the Bench of Bishops
And had audience of the Pope
It won't really be a problem
When at last my years are past
It's not what you know but who you know
That matters at the last.

NORMAN FRISKNEY

HUMAN CONDITIONAL

Born out of stardust, matter inanimate
Awakening first into fabric and form
Down through the ages from early Pre-Cambrian
And past mass extinctions a sentience is born.

Genes that we share with the rest of creation
For one is all life and life is all one
And next there emerges a clouded awareness
The timespan of which has so barely begun.

And so the newcomer, but lately perceptive
In so brief a span turned his gaze to the skies
With artefacts able to scan the beginnings
Ontology long before earth crystallised.

Tracking the signals from ten billion light years
Quasars outshining whole galaxies in light
Long travelled to bring him from primeval beacons
Symbols of spacetime emerging from night.
For out of the void of that singularity
A myriad of suns, nebulae and clusters were born
Whilst hydrogen transmuted down through to carbon
Could give to existence both substance and form.

Discerning now yet at the heart of the galaxies
Where matter's devoured and light cannot escape
Swept down the vortex to other dimensions
Where exotic laws of physics take shape.

But perforce, limitations within his perceptions
Evolved as he is, he can but comprehend
Only that which within circumscribed confines
Of ear, sight and touch or through reason extend.

So beyond this continuum in other dimensions
Although we have reached deep in space, back in time
There may lie beyond our dim apprehension
Realities of which we can never see sign.

Presumptuous those who would claim or give promise
Of houris in heaven or pie in the sky
Be they psychic or prophet or priest or predictor
Avowing it's theirs to both give or deny.

For man's but an infant, a child of the cosmos
As he looks to horizons remote from the shore
And on giants' shoulders, like Newton he ponders
The ocean of truth he has yet to explore.

SWEET MEMORY

Would that I could the years again
With happy heart and free
The labyrinthine lanes of life
Walk once again with thee.

But yet if I this question ask
Then lightly comes reply
That it is but sweet memory's task
To ope the inward eye.

NORMAN FRISKNEY

Weep then not one who left alone
Sweet memory tears will smother
The love and laughter we have known
Lives then on in the other.

GAUDY NIGHT

They came to thank the college for all that it had done
And commend its great good fortune in the Class of '41.
For some wines soon need drinking and are early past their best
And others lose their potency or never pass the test
But all agreed the Jesus Chateau bottled '41
Encapsulates perfection, for its class defers to none.

Alight full 50 years before with post-pubescent fires
Up from the Principality or sunny English shires
Meyrick scholars from their hayricks, bucolic boys from Wales
Coal dust in their turn-ups and beneath their fingernails
Leavened by the English left their Celtic country home
For the groves of Academe and the philosophy of Rome.

There were those who worked their socks off to become respected doctors
But other boys were soon marked down by the bulldogs and the proctors
Pursued by Deans of College for returning poor collections
With heavy bills for battels and excessive predilections
For ladies lurking in the lanes, or worse at Parsons' Pleasure
Until donnish disapproval was soon to get their measure.

For the ladies up at LMH wore stockings that were blue
And those who saw the tops of them were far between and few
Freshmen thought they had on offer something no one would refuse

But they wouldn't submit at Somerville or yield to them at Hugh's
And so for sublimation they played games and drank their ales
For those were days when they could still play Rugby down in Wales.

The war ended and returning to the body academic
Substituting martial forays for disputation and polemic
They next sought lifetime sinecures in College cures of souls
Whilst others sought salvation in more money grubbing roles
With perks at Unilever, Marks and Sparks or ICI
Preferring dining out with Mammon to pie up in the sky.

For there were those who went and did, whilst those who couldn't do
Departed for didactive jobs where assets don't accrue
Becoming dons or schoolmasters or similar humble creatures
And those who couldn't even teach endeavoured to teach teachers
Whilst others sought a richer but a less demanding fare
Living amid the fleshpots of a professorial chair.
So in their Celtic twilight or their darkling English dusk
They gathered there for dinner, attired in deep subfusc
To celebrate survival of 50 glorious years
Surrounded by good company of undergraduate peers
Each one of whom had weathered far less well than they had done
But to who all of them gave thanks to Jesus Floreat collegium.

A CAUTIONARY WORD FOR 18/21

At half a score and eight today
You're deemed to be discreet
To go to pubs or sit upon

A Parliamentary seat
See naughty films or go to jail
Or leave the family nest
Or back a horse and lose your all
Right down to shirt and vest.

For Shakespeare in The Winter's Tale
Tells us with every care
To watch our fathers and pay heed
To wisdom and grey hair
So woe betide the wayward wight
Who reaches one and twenty
To find that in the years between
The old man has learned plenty.

PARADISE NEARLY REGAINED

(with apologies to Messrs Goldsmith, Shakespeare, Wordsworth and Milton)

As gold gives way to greying hair
And slow erosion of the years
Takes from our eyes the light of youth
And the world's cares about us crowd
Now burn the fires low.
Limp lies that organ once so proud
Which once the startled world surprised
And now its muted note no longer gravity
And Time's winged chariot defies
But soft, as autumn leaves about us fall
Toccata, fugue and fantasy around us sound
And music of the spheres

Delights as that of other sphericules declines
And notes of that sweet Eden of our days
In paradise regained around us plays.

A WIDOW'S HUMP

I am a golfer's widow
And very glad of that
He wakes me up at crack of dawn
And dons his golfing hat
He brings me up a cup of tea
And lays my breakfast tray
Makes no demands upon me
And clears off for the day.
As soon as he has shut the door
I go to sleep and dream
Of big, athletic, handsome men
All bronzed and tall and lean
And then I rise and lounge about
Have coffee with the girls
Pop up to town with Hubby's cash
Buy dresses, shoes and pearls.

And when at dusk he trails home
All caked with mud and dirt
I say 'Oh, I've had such a time
I've washed your dirty shirts
And made the beds and cooked your meal
I've slaved and slaved away
While you've enjoyed yourself out
I've been alone all day.'

So conscience-struck they take us out
To talk and drink and dine
Spending all their hard-earned cash
On costly food and wine
It's good to be so cherished
For they'll never really find
As we gaze up with eyes admiring
What's really in our minds.

SOCIAL INSECURITY

I'm going down to see him at the surgery today
No, I haven't an appointment, but I'll catch him at the door
I know that when he sees me he won't dare send me away
And in an emergency that's what we pay them for.

It's this intermittent pain that just comes on and then goes off
As I told him only earlier in the week
When he gave me a prescription for my irritating cough
And I had that nasty spot upon my cheek.

Then I've got to make another trip to tackle Darren's Head
Those teachers just don't understand the lad
He can't help it if he's missed so many days off school
We just had to keep him home to help his dad.

They ought to make an effort to help the boy catch up
They do not understand that he's not strong
So I'm going down to see them to really sort them out
Some people just don't know they're in the wrong.

It's a good thing we've the time to settle all these things
You really need more hours in the day
Yes he's had to leave his job again, it never really brings
Enough money in, with all these bills to pay.

Still, it's better on security and housing benefit
And we still claim our dad's pension since he died
I know you'll keep your mouth shut or you'll drop us in the shit
About the decorating Bert does on the side.

NAME DROPPING

We had captured Rome in '44, and so with every hope
That the war might soon be over we had an audience with the Pope.
So we went into the Vatican and there we stood in line
As the Pontiff said a kindly word and crossed each with a sign
Standing there with other officers of the British Infantry
Were His Holiness the Pope, the Cardinals and me.

Back at Oxford for the Gaudy at the Principal's at three
Among distinguished company for sandwiches and tea
Awaking failing memories with fading old contemporaries
I could hardly bear to wait to discuss affairs of state
With the Principal, the Vice Chancellor, the Prime Minister and me.

At a Royal Society soiree in the groves of academe
I was privileged with others to be presented to the Queen
And as she walked along the line of guests I slightly bent my knee
And for a fleeting moment it was just the Queen and me.

I know that when my time is come and I am called away
To meet those of distinction, who each within his day
Changed history, ruled nations, was of international fame
And who in their various stations were illustrious, of acclaim
We'll sit before a roaring fire, nitric acid in our tea
And there'll be a sting in all our tails, Mephistopheles, Beelzebub and me.

PASSPORT TO PARADISE

In idleness, sweet idleness
He'd laze his life away
In torpor and in stupor
As he lay abed all day.
He'd loaf and lounge and loiter
In sleepiness and sloth
As in a supine stupor
Dissipating days of youth.

But soon in manhood's mirror
He observed himself with pride
Who could fail in admiration
Of one so set aside
From those of no distinction
Of low degree and dim
Whose speech betrayed their origins
As they looked up to him.

In his prime he soon surrendered
As a lustful libertine
To the joys of dissipation

VERSATILE VERSE

And practices obscene
Ravishing and defiling
With unrestrained, unbridled fire
Debauching and seducing
A libidinal satyr.

But now, espying others
Who had more than he himself
He looked upon with envy
At the hard acquired pelf
Of those who'd worked their socks
Whilst he had lazed all day
For vanity, sloth and lechery
There is a price to pay.

So now in his adulthood
False witness he would bear
To beggar any neighbour
Who would cross his path or dare
As the trees of their maturity
Bore the fruits of righteous youth
As with malice and malignancy
He manipulated truth.

Well now into corruption
He amassed a tidy sum
In assets salted overseas
Where the taxman's fiats don't run
Unscrupulous and miserly
He laundered it abroad
Adept at double dealing
In deceit, bad faith and fraud.

NORMAN FRISKNEY

So now as age began to tell
Engorged with food and wine
As gormandising gluttony
Began to give a sign
That his wanton dissipation
And devoted saturnalia
Would bring warnings from his doctors
Of constitutional failure.

Deciding that the time was come
To repent his life of sin
He swore his full contrition
Whilst hoping that he'd win
Thro' supreme unction, absolution
And a pass to paradise
He vowed that he had put aside
All wickedness and vice.

And so when death had claimed his soul
He reached the other place
Came reply as for admission
He claimed a state of grace
You're not Protestant nor Catholic
Mohammedan or Jew
We require the proper documents
And take the chosen few.

If there's a moral to this tale
Then surely it must be
Make sure you've bought your ticket
Franked for eternity

For the world is full of choices
Of religion, sect and class
But admission's never guaranteed
Unless They've stamped your pass.

PRIMARY COLOURS

On the canvas of the contract
Colours yellow, blue and red
In combine or in contrast
When each pair is newly wed
In lifescapes as in landscapes
As each picture slowly forms
Some show brush-strokes subtly blending
Others dark, presaging storms.

For these are coarse creations
And the colours angry, stark
And skies darken and shades deepen
As the artists make their mark
Whilst the paper that was pristine,
Lit with newly nuptial light
Becomes a storm-swept seascape
Of foreboding, fear and night.

But there are other paintings
In this gallery of life
Where the tones and colours blending
Between the couples, man and wife
Create a picture showing

For all who come to see
Beauty both for the beholders
For the artists, harmony.

THE TREES

Side by side they grew, thriving and prospering
The two young trees, as the sap rose and fell
With the slow heartbeat of the seasons.
Leaf burst and fall, winter sleep and summer sun,
Growing ever upwards into a canopy from which
Their progeny was spread in their joint image.

Whilst unseen, though likened to each other above the earth
Below the roots entwined, entangled into joint support
And when the gales came, each bent with the other
Withstanding year on year together all the storms of life could bring.

And then, one day, many seasons on, their seed themselves now bearing fruit
There came a great gale. The two old trees, roots still entwined,
Fell in the weight of wind and lay together on the woodland floor.

So when that we upon our woodland floor lie side by side
With roots entwined may others who are left
Relate that they gave others succour, shade and shelter
Through their joint commingling and their love.

TO KATHLEEN

I am much less than I would be
The word unsaid, the song unsung
The best that I would be for thee
Too often is the deed undone.

And what is past yet incomplete
Is cloth that we can ne'er repair
Whilst future's fabric, gossamerlike
Floats yet unspun in summer air.

For flesh is grass and man the bloom
That withers in a fleeting day
And ever fleeting time won't stop
For he who can't himself assay.

Know then thyself, ephemeral
Forever's captured in an hour
And friendship, love, so vulnerable
Is yet more lasting than a flower.

LONG LOVE

Long love's a voyage on boundless sea
Which storms and shallows all defy
For what binds fast twixt me and thee
Transcends the beauty of the eyes.

Long love is like a garden fair
Planted in youth with hope and joy
Which day by day in coupled care
Holds beauty years can ne'er alloy

And at time's end for me and thee
Who fifty years past was my bride
In eternity's sweet company
I would that you were at my side.

PER AMOR AD ASTRA

Come live with me and be my love
Where rocket motors soar above
And roar beyond Canaveral
Their melancholy madrigal

And I will make thee reservations
For interplanetary stations
Lest statesmen turn our fondest hopes
To radioactive isotopes

And there beyond the stratosphere
We'd build a better base, my dear
If such a flight thy fancy moves
Leave then with me and be my love.

VERSATILE VERSE

BETTER THAN RUBIES

Four decades long, and yet so seeming short
First love's young dream, a comely bride,
Rejoicing by her as he caught
Such light of radiance at his side
And in sweet song for one another given
There never was a better bargain given.

Yet follows now a second span of years
The tender bonds consolidate their hold
Annealed and tempered by life's joys and tears
Friends, family, their love extends, enfolds
And in sweet song for one another given
There never was a better bargain driven.

As then into the third decade they move,
The world with all its wonders and its woes
Brings yet a new dimension to their love
As each more like unto each other grows
And in sweet song for one another given
There never was a better bargain given.

So now with full and forty years complete
As hand clasped hand in hand, they mark the day
And bonds of love extend yet as they meet
With those who share life's journey all can say
In sweetest song and in all truth accept
There never was a better bargain sealed and kept.

NORMAN FRISKNEY

THE SUNDIAL

As slowly moves the shadow of the sun
To mark the passing hours of summer days
And all your garden flowers basked in light
Turn heads to follow in their dance of praise
These bounteous gifts of nature heaven sent
Are but custodians for short season lent.

Whilst all that in life's lottery befalls
As times of joy and sorrow alternate
Rejoice in sunshine, and when shadow falls
Remember, like the sundial's changing state
Both light and shadow each are blessings fine
To paint the profile of the soul divine.

FOR A SILVER WEDDING

No man's an island to himself complete
And each a part of all must ever be
And as time's ceaseless shuttle flies
The cloth that from love's thread derives
Compounds all else with thee.

And those with whom we marry, live and love
Within this swift short passing span of years
Is metal from life's furnace cast
Tempered by shared experience past
Of joys and hopes and fears.
And so as silver slowly turns to gold

Transmuted by life's subtle alchemy
Shine bright that others too may share
The love that each to other bear
This anniversary.

THE USHER'S TALE

A clerk there was of Catteford also
Who unto logyck hadde long ago
For he did have at his beddés heed
Full forty bookes clad in black and rede
Each day this clerke would he hie to schole
And teach sound learning and the gramar rule
Full wise was he in disputation sage
And in psycologie and yet the stage
Folk flockmeele came to hear his versatilitie
Ere he depart for more to Universitie.

Now had this clerke a fair and comely wife
Who he had wed and loved all her life
A woman she of many gifted parts
In cooking, learning and the finer Arts
Full filléd were her fingernails of clay
For she did pottes maken every day
At Stokéwell along the pilgrims' road
Hard by my Lord of Rochester's abode.
A Principal lived in this college fair
Wise in geographie, a learning rare
A woman sounde, of great and high degree
And goode whose name was called Rose Marie
Now Anne, this potter, lovèd her full well
Which brings me to this tale I have to tell

NORMAN FRISKNEY

THE TALE

It fell upon a certain Sabbath day
As from her hair she combèd out the clay
To make her way to church herself to shrive

A plan full goode and kinde she did contrive
To make a chambre pot of fulsome girth
Fashoned with clays best yet than Fulrés Earth
And blessed body of Saint John divine
Finished with glaze in curious desyng
To make a pris to this sweet Principal
When nexten came a college festival.

The feast of good Saint Blaize to whom we pray
Followed upon a Lenten holy day
This fulsome pot was placéd in the hall
And Rose Marie called now her clarkés all
To witness as she ersten was to sitte
And try for ease of comfort and of fitte
Uplift her overestye courtepy
And sat upon this pot fulle graciously
When on its bottom met her startled gaze
The malencolie face of goode Saint Blaize.
'Yvele it sitte' quod she and lept away
And brak in sherds this noiseme pot of clay
Whilst Anne the potter quailed as she did see
The darkling shades of full redunancie
With scholares sitting at her feet namoor
And places full of froward blackamoor.

Yet now my tale is done for this Marie
Was goode and full of Goddès sweet mercie
And Anne within her potterie does glaze
Her penitential pottes for goode Saint Blaize.

FORGIVE ME

Forgive me if I still trespass in your dreams
Nightmares shared once by light of common day
In war full fifty years ago, for yet it seems
That years between dissolve like mists away.
When only night could bring the balm
And sleep could close its curtain on the day.

Forgive me if I still trespass in your dreams
Those shades and shadows of so long ago
Those drifting, insubstantial scenes
That only we as sole survivors know.
Forgive, for as in night's long hours confine
You, in my dreams, can yet still enter mine.

TO LUCY AND KIARA ON REACHING EIGHTEEN

I am the voice that speaks to you
Down distant corridors of time
Whose genes you share with others too
In long ancestral common line
Converged from either side of Europe's civil wars
The folly of our fathers, mine and yours.

For you are loved and yet more loved
Who bring the healing's sheltering palm
To we once young, for mirrored in your eyes
Are images of love, the catharsis and the calm
That binds us all in Mankind's common weal
And seals it as a blessing and a balm.

ODE TO AN AGEING TENNIS PLAYER

Your frame is warped
Your strings are frayed
The net moth eaten and decayed
Dry rot your post has made corrupt
It soon will crumble into dust
Your balls are rotten with decay
The net cord rusts and flakes away
Grey is the sky and cold the rain
And tennis will not come again.
Despair you not, for yet the sun
Will shine and you shall be restrung
The mesh around your court rewired
And brand new balls shall be acquired
Your post, once limp, shall be restored
And stand erect with new net cord
With brand new gut, your frame put right
You'll play as well by day or night
As in the Elysian fields you'll sport
On God's eternal tennis court.

DANCING

It is good to get old together
For the total transcends the parts
Whilst the dance that we dance together
Echoes two close beating hearts

And tho' at some time one dancer
Must be left on the floor alone
As the beat of the fading music
Dulls down to a monotone.

But feel not bereft, you old dancer
For the music still plays on above
And the score is writ sweet in the heavens
For grief is the price paid for love.

A VISITATION

And in my dream the spirit came
Said 'Power have I for you to plan
That you may live your life again
From youth to age in its full span
And you may choose a time long past
In any place you may define
Or yet some era not yet cast
Which sleeps in future's womb of time.'

Then said I to the spirit bright
Long past or future I'd refuse

My own times yet again I'd walk
Along familiar paths I'd choose
Held hand in hand with one I love.
'That cannot be!' the spirit cried
As morning light dawned from above
And waking, she was by my side.

THE SPINNEY

When winter paints the garden white
And all the wood in silence sleeps
And trees are traceries of light
Which lace the sky as snowfall spreads
Its wedding gown with lavish love
Upon the canopy above.

Swift passing is snow's wedding dress
As sunshine ends its little day
And benisons of blossoms bless
As winter passes soft away
So shall our love renewèd be
Each season's anniversary.

ALL FLESH IS AS GRASS

Fear not that feared tomorrow
For I will always be beside
And though unseen to guard and guide
Yet ever present to dissolve your sorrow

For I was always there about you even 'ere we
So long ago until the seeds of destiny
Took root and then matured
Into that blessed tree that we together set
But little time must then needs pass
When we will once again united be
As wind that murmurs through the leaves
And scent of flowers and light and shadows on the grass.

YOUNG LOVE

Two faces profiled in soft candlelight
Gazing intent one upon the other
Across the table in this far hotel
Amongst the mountains, here for but one night.

Limited of pocket, yet devote
And doubly blessed with vigour of sweet youth
And doubly yet again by one another's presence
In their island, inviolate and remote.

Soft voices murmur from each table, drift
Across the room, but not from theirs,
Their eyes alone commune in silence
That sense that lies in lovers' gift.

And yet we need no lexicon, for we know
The music and the magic of their unspoken words
For we still speak that selfsame litany
A language which we too learned long ago.

NORMAN FRISKNEY

THE SECRET GARDEN OF FLOWERS

I dreamt of foxes wearing gloves
And cows all dressed in filmy slips
Whilst wandering lads declared their love
To ladies clad in gossamer lace.

And suckling bees their honey supped
By garden walls with flowers clad
Whilst kings and queens raised drinking cups
To maidens crowned with golden hair.

As hooded monks ate cheese and bread
With butter paddled into cups
A dog with wings to heaven rose
And mists of dreams swirled round my love.

As they dissolved and I awoke
My lips brushed soft upon her cheek
And fairer than those flowers of dreams
All twelve you may now find and seek.

www.ingramcontent.com/pod-product-compliance
Lightning Source LLC
Chambersburg PA
CBHW061346040426
4244CB0011B/3108